DROP
and
DAZZLE

DROP and DAZZLE

poems by
Peggy Dobreer

~ 2018 ~

Drop and Dazzle
© Copyright 2018 Peggy Dobreer
All rights reserved. No part of this book may be used or reproduced in any manner whatsoever without written permission from either the author or the publisher, except in the case of credited epigraphs or brief quotations embedded in articles or reviews.

Editor-in-chief
Eric Morago

Associate Editor
Michael Miller

Proofreader
Jim Hoggatt

Front cover photo & color design
Brendan Constantine & Katja Rigter

Back cover & author photo
Alexis Rhone Fancher

Book design
Michael Wada

Moon Tide logo design
Abraham Gomez

Drop and Dazzle
is published by Moon Tide Press

Moon Tide Press #166
6745 Washington Ave.
Whittier, CA 90601
www.moontidepress.com

FIRST EDITION

Printed in the United States of America

ISBN # 978-0-9974837-5-8

*For my beloveds.
You are the world of which I speak.*

CONTENTS

Foreword by Nicelle Davis 8

I. Billows Start to Spread

Climbing the Moment of Birth 14
Scarlet Billows Start to Spread 15
Serving Fresh Fish 16
Rituals 17
Intaglia 18
Her Name Was Tiffany, or Else It Was Piper 19
Retro Causation 21
Genesis 22
Karma as First Mode of Transportation 23
Exquisite Harmonics 24

II. Fade to Glory

Hello, Little Fish 29
Edison & Co. 30
The Hands of Glory 31
The Hoax 32
Her Holiness of the Torch 33
Is There a Doctor in the House? 34

III. Permanence & Pain

Periwinkle, Permanence, and Pain 39
A Dress to Die For 40
Kama Sutra 41
Choosing the Right Word 42
Ruby Wind 43
Mortality 44
A Love Like Hair on Fire 45
Plotting 46
Two-Headed Heart 47
Ashes to Ashes 48

IV. Scene Play

Scene: Lullaby and Aubade 53
Scene: The Disclaimer 54
Scene: The Lovers...55
Scene: The Wilderness 56
Scene: The Reminder 57
Scene: No Words...58
Final Scene: The House 59

V. The Other Side

Yixing, Heating the Clay Pot 63
Xu San Li 64
Dumpling 65
Chinaberry Credenza 66
Words Saved to Use in a Poem 67
Reminder Notes to Self on Writing...68
Astronomical Units of Flight 69
Glorious Tango..70
The Dazzling 71

About the Author 73
Acknowledgements 74

FOREWORD

Poetry, at its best, gives people a way to find joy in life's great hardships. It doesn't seek to simplify, but rather exemplify the moments when we become fully alive. This is what Peggy Dobreer does in her collection *Drop and Dazzle*. The title makes reference to how as a child Peggy was taught to hide under her school desk in order to avoid the effects of possible atomic bomb attacks. We are all dazzled by life, no matter how impossible the circumstances. Peggy's poetry makes the impossible possible. Love, with all its dazzling and dark facets, is made possible as we drop our defenses and surrender to a life fully lived.

In the initial section, "Billows Start to Spread," love is in motion. With love as a verb, earth in the kiln turns flesh-colored. The father tries to dance himself to death after returning from war, while the daughter pretends to get drunk on Shirley Temples. The world is a game of Red Rover, waiting for tomorrow to come on over. Our necks are gripped by perfection; call that perfection mother. Every Genesis can be found at a funeral. When the mouth finally stops talking, it becomes a violet.

The poems of this first section billow in that large (yet private) mimicry of wishing on dandelions. In the destruction of one form, many others are born. And so begins our adventure into *Drop and Dazzle*.

The collection continues with, "Waiting on Glory." In love's purgatory, life is a carousel. We make things up to avoid feeling down. The electrician is blind to the haunting romance of candlelight. The losses of miracles are mourned on a rope. The whole affair with faeries has been dismissed. Albino cobras and golden panties are singing for a forever. Doctor's drink Wild Turkey and refuse to garden.

In other words, love disappoints; we wait anyway. The waiting becomes its own ride—a carousel; we make countless returns for glory.

The third section, "Permanence & Pain," has us dress without fear in tattooed roses. A nakedness falls open and we know pleasure for pleasure's sake. The poems ask: *when were we humble enough to taste crème brulee?* When did we last risk the double-down of desire? Our sails threadbare but willing to bear the movement—when did we last love?

These are brave poems; they skip from one to another, without ever touching ground. "Scene Play," the fourth section, is an Odyssey—if you have forgotten the way to love, these poems will draw you a map. From scene to scene, we see whom we dare to hold. Lovers are water on the belly. Write it all down on the bottom corner of each page—all the blank space above represents all that's been given up.

What is given up for love is the shore.

The collection concludes with "The Other Side," where we drink tea in a snow storm—the beginning of the world is unknown as the last fallen flake. Say meteorites and mean passion, or pain. Pull life towards you—be gravity and allow yourself home. Shadow can't survive the night—yet through poetry, we can still see.

It won't take you long to realize that many of the phrases in this introduction are lifted from the actual collection. That is the way with good writing—there is nothing to add, only ways to admire. *Drop and Dazzle* does just as the title claims—it awes the reader into surrender—it turns the world into wonder.

Nicelle Davis
Los Angeles, 2018

In my deepest wound, I saw your glory and it dazzled me.
—St. Augustine

Out of used furniture, she made a tree.
—Anne Sexton

I.
BILLOWS START TO SPREAD

Climbing the Moment of Birth

What I might confess are secrets,
packed like clay into kiln, hardened
fast in the bowl of the breath.

What I must divulge are pinks.
Sinew. Soft tissue damage, flesh
and bone stalled in the act of being.

What I remember is when fluorescent
hit my eyes I was blinded to the room,
its dull linoleum, metal cabinet, the bed.

Permanence dismantled in a litany of instruments,
each in its own tongue. Mothers of Russia
and Poland, fathers of Egypt and Spain,

spinning out from the Lion's Mouth,
cradling *knadle,* fleeing *Pogroms*. What
I understand is tenderness, rendered

hand to cheek, cheek to lung, to breath.
The way love presents in a wilderness
of birth, infirmary dank.

On a war-tired base, under desert skies,
the only thing I remember of my birth
is the smell of death.

Scarlet Billows Start to Spread

I grew up learning to eat properly
at The Brown Derby, The Duck
Press and The Pacific Dining Car.
We'd sit next to a dance floor where
there was one, the sound of a kitchen
un-pleasing to father's ear. I learned
how skin could crawl from my father.

I grew up singing lounge music,
making up for Daddy's infractions
at The Palladium after the war. He
wanted to dance himself to death,
and mother never broke a sweat.

I grew up behaving with Duke and
Josie at Dino's on the strip. I drank
Shirley Temples with my three perfect
sisters in patent leather shoes, crinoline
itching elbows, grosgrain waist bands
cinching smiles into place.

I grew up cringing at Duke's lizard grin,
frozen in time between verses of *Old
Sukey Tawdry, and Miss Lotte Lenya,*
I was always waiting between sets for
the *shark with pearly teeth big…
Look out. Old Macky's back in town.*

Serving Fresh Fish

I am from spinning
from kickball in the cul-de-sac
I am from ally
I am from free falling down
curd cuts through plaster
I am from chill hid in basement
door unbolted
I am from avocado fruit
held in the arms
I am from below sea level
King Neptune was
His staff in hand
get caught up
on the strand
And it is not
I am
Junior Lifeguards
bury washed-up jelly fish
I am from
I am from waves
horizons
I am from sun
take off layers, oil
I am from transistor radios
and sails
Waves meeting
A havoc of ocean
splashes
I am from two fish flopping
I am fresh

in circles and rolling down hills
till streetlights come on
ally oxen...
tree climbing up when
flies up brackish stairwell
smell of damp earth
above my head
supped off thick black skins
of the mother pear
and just above third eye
my invisible childhood friend
we'd ride the tram from P.O.P.
with beatnik lesbians in tattoo galleries
Grandmother didn't like it Not one bit
because of the way they dress she said
from Bubby's rules
Keep things safe
recycle aluminum
picking up for others
rushing in and rinsing out
glooming in the mist
cut through clouds
tinted with iodine
on blankets
beyond break rocks
at the top of the berm
foams between my toes
up my thighs
out of school
from loving you?

Rituals

My mother's hands were slender,
secretly slipping Virginia Slims
from the pack, hiding her long
smoky palms in the folds of her apron
while kissing Father hello. The way
she tucked loose hairs at her nape back
into last Friday's French twist.

She knew what her curls called for,
salt and pepper since fourteen,
coarse like fresh ground. Tamed on
a steel rat comb and an aerosol of Aqua Net.
Our mother sat at her dressing table,
on a silver speckled hassock. Vinyl
beneath a satin gown, she carefully
spit her curls onto paper squares before
tying up her pink triangle hair net for the night.

She slept on satin pillows, hands palm
to palm beneath one cheek. What is it she
holds between them, I thought? My mother
could keep a confidence at all cost, raised
four girls to be seen looking good but
not heard. On waking each day, one numb
hand always wheezed to the other, *I can't
breathe. Let me out from under here.*

Intaglia

What the neighbors swear they don't know
could fill a wind tunnel used to mimic
weightlessness on the way to the moon.
The way a lamp near the window throws
shadows across a curtained lens
inviting moths.

When the hum of morning carves itself
into a memory, you leave your books behind,
carry a sticky fist of glimpses tainted
by the sum of what never seems to add up
in the end. *What end?* you say, offering lilies
to Our Lady of Perpetual Faith.

That which is stolen knows no diameter, weight
is undetectable where elements of heaven
are found etched in, dug up from the past,
revealed as glyphs, a mystery *minimalis*.
It's true. We are stardust, hardly a thought,
a fleeting note on its way to a verse or
a song.

It sends the salmon running. How can such
a tall order be filled in a nuclear sea?
Stars gleam through the eye of the Milky Way.
The neighbors are salmon in starlight.
A wind tunnel bellows behind the barn.

Her Name Was Tiffany, or Else It Was Piper
after "Nuclear Gospel" by Kenny Ortega

Once she smoked on the steps of the main library.
Twice she went to England with a sailor.
She was a stand-in, an extra, a punk kid in an alley.

Once she was the star of a whole show
and found she didn't care. She was a concierge—
made appointments, collected gratuities.

Once she was a chef, a prison tutor, model citizen.
She was highly employable, desirable, always
on the go, coming back, finding another gig, no problem.

Once she was "the farmer's wife," Alfred Hitchcock,
a one act, very short lived. Once she worked
in a center for organs.

And pianos. An oddly messy job, things got lost
in multiples of three. Usually inversions.
Always, her responsibility.

But once ago, she had been a girl with bells on the beach,
a jeweler, joiner, dancer, healer. Once she saw
the jig was up, and went in again anyway.

She had no sense, couldn't use the brain god gave her.
But she had felt the arms of god around her.
And once in a while she lost her faith.

But even before that, on a vineyard in Sonoma,
she was lead singer in a band called The Promise Land.
She rode BART in paint-splatted overalls. Had purple hair

with a wide pink stripe. She practiced
to the white roar as the train rolled under the bay.
Your friends are all crazy and you don't know why.

*They've been running in circles as long as you've
known them, they've been trying to get married,
get rich or get high, or get by.* And on her day job…

she climbed six-story scaffolds in the sun, painted rich
contrasting colors in clean lines around window frames
in the windy city. She was strong, and fearless then.

And the Presidio lay at the paws of the Golden Gate.
And she kept singing, and the bay looked small
from up there. And the ocean went on and on…

*But now the time is running out for playing games
with those that bend your mind. You'll be done for, if you
don't run for the door, and leave the friends behind, before*

*you lose your mind. Run forget your lover. Run forget
your strife. Run, run for cover. Run for your life.*

Retro Causation
after Maxine Hong Kingston

She's got some nerve, oh boy,
some call her the maker of the Procrustean bed.

Don't be too smart, too strong, too epiphanied.
Temporary infertility is to be expected in art.

She has the bad itch. Is restless as water,
but looks cool as crinoline outside.

Inside, sharp as a shark's tooth and galled as glory
on a Sunday morning in the front pews.

If you are alienated in your own house
how can your wings ever unfurl?

How can the moth of your flurried past
shield the shape of your history from your future?

An act of love today can save a long lost life
on an ancient battlefield, in a country as yet unnamed.

Genesis

      In the word
was the beginning.
        And the beginning was
new. Except of course that it could
        have happened.Like force,

      it has no opposition
until something moves against it.
      Then all force leads
to more. Escalation
      is inevitable, inexorable.

mineral or phenomenal, floral or
      faunal, your way or the anyway.
It makes no difference so long as
      lips and hungers are
married to art and soul. Sole.

      There it is. The word used
for fish, and foot bottom.
      Once I missed the sticky tar
from the ocean, till my down facing
      dog looked into a mirror. Once

the sound of his voice was as
      necessary as the rain that followed.
Once the gutters all emptied
      downstream, their slosh and flush
but a river headed to sea. See the tiny

      ships of fate dappling the crowded
bay, their bright flapping masts?
      The giant babies inside us
cannot help but pluck them up with
      clumsy thumbs, the unsuspecting
little sailors falling free.

Karma as First Mode of Transportation

Mars was my home planet then.
I wore a white uniform and counted
pills like stars. Side effects must be
read later, otherwise no one would
ever dare. *Was I an abductee,* you ask,
a foraging savior, bargaining for grace?

It's hard to know. Memories escape
like convicts with tools. I meant to
bring water to my friend without hips
but her feet beat mine to the door.
I wanted to stand out without shouting,
returned a violet, no mouth.

Exquisite Harmonics

What is exquisite
    is the breaking of china
        splash against tile
    bright tones of glass

What is exquisite
    is the tango of Kali
        The savory statement
    of unsung stanzas
The brain quenching
    fire of mouths

Migration of the herd
    to the gate of the mind
        Throne of the flesh
            that lights up the eye
                Arc of the rib to
                      the bone in the soup

What is exquisite
    is a memoir of the body
        A vibratory tonic of
    connective harmonics
        guiding chants that
            can't be extinguished

What is exquisite
    is this limitless unleadening
        alchemy of Ganesh on our sleeves

In the breath
    of the opening cage
        the rush to rhapsody's rest
            in the eyes of the hawk
                on the wings of a loon
                    who light this way and
                        fill these forests
with words.

II.
FADE TO GLORY

Hello, Little Fish

I still can't see the sombrero for the trees. Trees, carved into horses, that is. In full dressage, in flight, that is. Painted and gilded. The way they go up and down. A carousel is a circus. Two swans glide by and now I'm making things up. I always make things up so close to sleep. Not sure how I keep getting away with it. Still I imagine a cup of strong coffee, or a nice rare steak. But I cannot locate the listed coffee pot or the unlisted cow. A penguin is listed, but has not made herself known. Do penguins speak at all? How do they call back their young? If I can't have another child, a steak, or a cup of Joe for the ride home, a candy cane and tiny fish will have to do.

Edison & Co.

There is usually one electrician in any small crowd, a guy who never looks in a mirror. He thinks mirrors are dangerous and may lead to obsessions and fear of ghosts. Ghosts are always lurking, that much is certain, but they can't be illuminated without igniting their own reflections in the glass. Legend has it that once a candle is lit, the literati can be seen assembling in the mirror over the mantel but not in the room. Those present are instantly filled with bravado and know their seeing to be final. The electrician goes on about his business fusing wires and making things light up. He is immune to candlelight. He has no interest in romance. He looks in the mirror with his one blind eye.

The Hands of Glory

The Tragedy of Donkey Row tells the legend of a stolen handkerchief from around a dead man's neck. When the execution crowd disbursed, they mourned the loss of the miracle, maybe more than the life of the man on the rope. They wandered away, and regrouped in a hotel lobby across the square. The paramount importance of the handkerchief became quite clear as the unsuccessfully gallowed man stood slowly and broke out in a pox from crown to chest. Some women ducked behind curtains of nervous laughter. Others disappeared shaking their heads and whispering. But it should be noted that deep in the folds of that kerchief was a message. It revealed that a mole, on the left breast of a girl, enabled her to choose any man she desired. By authority of this belief, it was assumed she would be rendered irresistible for evermore.

The Hoax

Scientists have found a faerie skeleton—so like a tiny human child, but hollow boned and winged for flight. Also reported are sightings of interspecies play going on in the liquid wild. The humpback and bottlenose are playing piggyback on the surf. And now, a whole barrow of faerie bones was discovered, apparently, undisturbed for centuries.

Tossing and sliding from slant snout to sea splash, cetaceans celebrate migration with a romp around the bay. Meanwhile, an official Scientific American photo shows a grayish faerie fossil, displayed in a pair of white-gloved hands? The coats have conferred, and now concur. The whole affair has been dismissed.

Her Holiness of the Torch

It costs a lot of money to look this cheap.

    —Dolly Parton

Medusa de Dolly Lama has some big old sutras, daddy. With spools of poisonous albino cobras for hair. A curling mass of steamy snow bled snipers at her scalp. Draped in velvet robes, she takes her place on fourteen carat cushions spun from the tossed jewels of greater gods and lesser goddesses. She seats herself on a raised pallet in perfect lotus posture. Standing in front of her, you might catch a glint off her golden panties if you hold real still and gaze slightly to the west with your deserving intact. Look how she sits so serene, fingers rested in mudras on her knees, her spirit sailing an unsalted sea, from 9-5, with that wild mane of serpents spinning incantations, seeking next prey, entwining infantries on advance, while Medusa de Dolly waits for a message under the weight of her white mane, lowers her register to sing once more, till it raises the hair on all our hopes... And I... E... I.... will always love you.

Is There a Doctor in the House?

A voice rang out in the restaurant. A man fell. People pushed their plates away. Was it the food? No one made a move. Sirens grew loud and stopped outside.

My Mother always said, *Marry a doctor*. She did the second time. It worked well for all of us. She had a murmur from a teenage fever that turned her hair gray at fourteen. *Salt and pepper,* he insisted. *Salt and Pepper.* She was told, *no children with that heart*. Had four. That was Mother.

A doctor gets up, makes rounds, wears a suit coat, a lab coat, a surgery gown, a hounds-tooth smoking jacket, and a wool cap in winter that his Ma sent from Baltimore. A doctor might grow a beard in autumn, have a whirl in politics, drink Wild Turkey. A doctor won't garden, not even water the lawn. He calls Sam. Gives him good work after internment. A doctor may even overpay, long after a man can do the hard work. Bend and shuffle, bend and shuffle, after all those years, like family in the garden. Sam came till he could no longer. The patio stairs still have no railing.

The EMT's could not revive him. Defib paddles failed. After the body bag was zipped, and they gathered to choose the box; after all those years he carried his black bag to bedsides in the dark, there was no doctor on the premises as his life slumped away. Whether you marry him or not, there is never a doctor in the house when you need one.

III.
PERMANENCE & PAIN

Periwinkle, Permanence, and Pain

You purchase pain with all that joy can give and die of nothing but a rage to live.

—Alexander Pope

I would ask for blue ink. Elegant and
        pale as Santa Fe skies, color of my eyes.
                People feel comfort when a person wears
        the color of their eyes.

A flourish that points
        to bones. The needle over them is
                unforgiving. Make mine a paisley
        splay on fleshy mounds. Merely
a nod to bones.

They carry our canvas upright, berth
        it low for sleep. Body fluids rise to
                needle pressure, puncture points,
        perilous and permanent. In the stain
of ink that knows my hands are stories to be told.
        A single artist bears my totem
                in his squiddy grip.

But if I had no fear of pain or death,
        I would choose a full corset tattoo. Roses
                in bloom over each hip, a heart of lace
        below the nape, the garment's gait
of stays and bones stippled across my ribs.

Breasts are lifted to admirable heights by
        the bawdy bustier, tightly laced in a
                stiffened stricture that shields breath
from lung. A firm cinch at the waist,
        the shine of leather, touch of silk, the
                claws of net on a bustled bossy posture
        that cannot be confused with any other girl.

A Dress to Die For

Parachutes have risen
and structures of fashion
have shifted in the foyer.

Prestigious and versatile,
the concierge collects
luxury gifts. She drinks
the beverage before her,

sucks air too loud to sigh.
A carnage of orchids
dries on Spanish tile. A red
pepper turns in the bowl.

The room yawns and fragments
of this odd assemblage fall off
the tongues of the terrace. No
word is offered to frame

reflections found in the lobby mirror.
The solstice swaggers the turn of
the screw to her jaw. A concert of anarchy
plays on her dress falling open just
above the knee.

Kama Sutra

You rock my Kama Sutra
with an intensity that
awakens my propensity
for a tango and the taste
of crème brûlée.

The sweet of your nothings
on the nape of my pleasure
rarifies the atmosphere and
clarifies the nature of my
nefarious feminine treasures.
Under your spell I become
a creature of emotion-filled
oceans of smoldering potions
pouring into the channels
of my star-eyed nature.

I am temporarily blended
into the mending together
of milk and will of
body and bones come
bubbling up in anticipation
of our one-on-one coming
undone in ways of two
become one.

We are humbled back as
we stumble into the
mumbled surrender of that
which overcomes us
and numbs us to our
comings and goings to
the hard-nosed hum-drum of
things we now have showing.

You rock my Kama Sutra,
with an intensity that
awakens my propensity
for a tango and the taste
of crème brûlée.

Choosing the Right Word

                It may be canopy,
carpet, canoe. When you're near,
        I call it safe harbor.
Rest in the slip.
      At times, it is tide
pools. Swallows me random,
        in wakeless whirling and falls,
                comes spilling double down.

            Maybe it's a pallet,
something to carry us. All this time,
      I thought it was a wheel. Spinning, spinning
best beloved, our gold threads stitching
        up my sheets. I will
            iron this pain till it's smooth.

            Maybe it's a room, love,
where discards dapple the floor.
        Garments strewn about, all-the-better
to know ourselves, the bright details
        of our skin. And the turn of our sleep,
            vistas that flutter back of lids.

            Maybe it's a whole house,
wherein we take our hair off. Put on our
        berries and plumes. Wear them out, as
if we owned the place. As if plush paths
        were laid open under
                our feet, step-by-step.

Ruby Wind

Indentured,
  your storm slurs
    against my weathered bow.

    My sails are threadbare,
  my hull rusty, adrift at
the predator's shore.

Come ye, pirate
  my decks, but with
    covered eye open.

    For I will fill your mast
  with my ruby wind, and you
will become precious in my cup.

Mortality

On the westside of the island,
a man carved a woman's body in sand.

It was so real that when I saw it through
the legs of the gathered bathers,

I thought someone had drowned.
I thought it might be me, because

of the taste of lake in my mouth,
ropes of reeds caught in my throat.

I checked. But my breath was there
becoming deeper, more pronounced,

the way breath will in the presence
of a body without one gasp left.

A Love Like Hair on Fire

How do we know what the bone-faced girl
will do next? This is how she bandages
the antlers of her thirst. This is how she lays
them at the threshold. How she moves
her hooves to step on the isthmus,
wade in the overspill.

There is a laying on of hands, like the tock
of the astronomical clock. How it reverberates
through brick-still innards. There is stroke
without tarry. There is easy leaving.
There is difficult listening, estranged
continuity. There is another bowl of herbs
and roots warming on the stove.

How I have been girded against our curried
rapture. A muslin vision. A weave so tight
even a tear cannot seep into the hardened
arteries of diction. Both of us tied by tongue
and promise.

How we keep building small tract houses,
where one love is abandoned, another points
home. Imagine this moment, or that. Now.
Or now. We wistfully implement pleasure,
our common denominator. The body knows
its own mesh, its perfect metal. You finish
your soup. A single bowl.

Plotting

I've been in the nook since you left.
We are cropped short in hot bolts.
Not lightning from clouds, but like

some errant charge from underground,
conduction of the lower vales. Look
how capable we are, how we lead

on descent. Slippered Sherpas
of severance. Feet turned out in dismay,
an impaired odyssey, their bolted gates.

We bury the bones in the children's plot,
where cherubim and headstones
lie close enough together

for the children we once were
to skip from one to another, without
ever having to touch the ground.

Two-Headed Heart

This is how it feels to have these bright pages
torn from the book of our days.

How it is to have the mortal coil wound so tight
its tensile fails, becomes

bannister without stairs, ballet *barre* without
first position or final *adagio*.

This is how it feels to fail. A simple sport of
strength or stamina. Speak or step.

Punt or recover. Extend or redact. Remember
push-me—pull-you pet? Two-headed giraffe,

front paws in Liberia, and also Sierra Leone.
Crimea, and also Ukraine. Israel

and Palestine, God or state, stay or go. This
is how it feels when morning meets

a lollygagging moon, winter white in a hot blaze
of sky. Like it forgot where it was going.

Ashes to Ashes

The world
is hurtful
and stupid.

Don't be
the world.

—Leigh White

So, here's the view, the breeze, the pulse
in your throat.

—Ellen Bass

The world wants to bury you.
Under a pile of leaves, or
an avalanche of snow or news.
It doesn't matter.

It won't care if your hair is perfect,
if you're punctual, or too late
to hold the reservation. There will be
no excuses when the world wants
what the world always wants.

The world always wants to bury you,
if you take your hands from ten and two,
bind your feet to make them small. If you
roll your points over, or move your money
to try to get more. If you're good at math,
but poor at finance. If you bet on others,
but never give your love a decent go.

The world will weigh you down with
impossible possibilities you can't possibly
meet. It won't care about your childhood,
your artistic statement, or the one
from the bank.

But it doesn't want to see you suffer.
So, the world will tell you to go, ask
you not to call. It will unfriend your spirit
and cause you to burn like rubber, to hop
like a maggot out to lunch.

The world will eat you like a snack.
It will toss your keepers and keep
tossing your losses till you're flat
on your back. And when you're gone,
the world will bury you again—

or it will have you cremated for
a fraction of the cost. You can have
your bones scattered over mountains,
or spread out to sea. You can finally
forget the world, return unto earth.

IV.
SCENE PLAY

Scene: Lullaby and Aubade

You rose quietly from my arms in Decatur. I didn't hear the door close. The key is the bond. Be of ours. Here I am your servant. You are my slave. I am the boss of you. You are my king, sir. I am jester. You are laureate. I am husband. You are fellow. I am girl child. You are real man. There are desks, two, or three. I build the fort. You lay down the law. We are all of these.

Scene: The Disclaimer

Lub-double cries in Jurassic rhythms. O, for the retouch, the pleasure. Deliveries whoosh by. You are action, fountain, an odyssey. A live concerto. Here goes. Perfected, a conscious galaxy, obedient memory. Believe somewhere between monkey thought and rhyming laughs. Between Georgia and a lobster's claw. Believe in dreamers who dance on astral, aurals, on cones and asphalt, the turning line. Crescendo on solid ground. What it takes to make us whole. The pieces we parse into, the halves, and have-nots, and whom we dare to hold.

Scene: The Lovers

I sang to the dream all day. Swaddled it in word blankets, but mostly sensation, water, a hand on my belly. The dream brightened in my arms where we slept, burrowed under my thigh for safe keeps. I went to the closet to put on your favorite dress. Even tighter now, I laid down in it, rolled over, held fast to the dream, soldered my faith to your chest.

Scene: The Wilderness

You have walled me again and I cannot bend the scaffolds steel beam. Crossties only an Escher could equal. I am propelled of best intent, a broken field of asphodels, buried in last rolled stones. I am hidden in night wings and Meriweather, a crimson goddess, tatted from cuff to chin, chosen from an old lunch counter in a two-bit town. *Nothing special about this girl,* you say. A young couple kiss tenderly on the screen overhead. This is a night to forget. I write it all down.

Scene: The Reminder

When I pass Camino Las Ramblas, I think of Barcelona, Christopher Columbus, the Nina, the Pinta, the Santa Maria. I think of Figueres, everything I missed, and all the way past the Castle Montjuïc, the pristine funicular, and the children, scampering, so dirty, joyous, running loose on the wharf. Then I pass the Goodyear blimp, tied by nose to the ground, basket drawn for the night. I think of Frankie. And the Hustler Casino billboard blinks, *let the hand do the talking*. When I pass Camino de Estrella, I think of John's new girlfriend. And the metal pins in Freddie's fragile arm.

Scene: No Words

Australopithecus is listed as first bipedal. But please, disregard this ancient evolution. So... where to start? Above my head is a sheer orb in a repercussive sky, a southern sky, a children's fire smoldering. Smogged and cerulean, a day sleeper, so like a baby floating face-down, bobble-headed and soft-spotted. Unbound in the body. The body is...outside of itself, astounded by the view.

Final Scene: The House

I see you there. Or I don't. Another room, brushes and paint. I leave the music alone. Surely damp winters come and we hunker in with our pads and stories. Surely, love moves pain. The rafters sing their achy song, the creaking wood, the crackling wind, croaking hours, frogs in the distance, crickets in the floorboards. Surely there is loss. Everything we gave up to get here. All the pretty little horses, patches of blue breaking open, the moon in its fullness, whether we see it or not. Tell me truly. What are you? What are you wearing?

V.
THE OTHER SIDE

Yixing, Heating the Clay Pot

*Tea ceremony is powerless. But it's also not such a bad thing either.
You should enjoy it while you can.*

    —Koushun Takami, *Battle Royale*

Beginnings are like snow storms.
    Who knows where the final flake will fall
        or how many days the white glaze will take
    to melt from the cake of town square?
Whenever I throw a party
    covenant arrives late.
        Maybe it's the loose joints
            at my elbows, the way blood
                travels through each and every cell
            to cross the plank between lobes.
    I plunge headlong
      into the draw for another breath.
One that holds the combination,
    fitly, like helium. Like rising
        to the occasion. Like lifted
            voice to sky. Or not having
                to say a thing. Just know,
                    slow and warm as tea.

Xu San Li

    If you dig a hole to China, it is known as—Point of One Hundred Diseases. Except in shuddering light along a bamboo river, the crowning point of infinite longevity. Stimulate often in circular fashion, many times throughout the day.

    To find it, cup your knee with the hull of your down-facing hands, fingers outstretched. Locate a small lagoon between ring and pinky, pool of skin lined by ridges of bone named for their fathers. One is Venerable Tibia, the other Master Fibula; twins, born of one marrow.

    But no matter their names. It is their station, their function in the whole of hominid carriage, directional flexible for femur of strength. In some cases, two bones are better than one.

    Massage mindfully, nine times clockwise. Say to yourself, nine is the number of fulfillment, 3 x 3, an expression of perfection, nine is completion, man in harmonium. This is motion marshaled in a stack of precious moments, endless as the bridge that splits us. How I have taught myself to visit you in marvel and haunting, like a newborn teaches herself to sleep, learns to love without lullabies.

    Now, it is of upmost importance to remember to counter the current after evening meal. To balance the beat, massage in the opposite direction. Dance with Compassionate Dragon. But not too near bedtime, as it could make sleep impossible. Could cause your clear eye to water away the hours, wink by wink.

Dumpling

Dim sum means dumpling, little heart,
meal of muses, and streaks of light.

When I say dim sum, I mean
streaks of light. And when I

say streaks of light, I mean
trails of meteorites on fire.

And when I say meteorites on
fire, I mean passion, pain.

And when I say pain, I mean
verse or song. I mean ready

to break. And when I say break,
I mean into verse or song.

And when I say verse or song,
I mean dim sum, little heart.

Chinaberry Credenza

*I've been listening so long / to the sound of wood splitting /
now I want to know / the sound wood makes when it's whole.*

—Renee Gregorio

A line of hand carved ridges
frames two sideboard cupboards.
Two long drawers with fleur de lis,
perfect for scrapbooks, a coffin flag
with 48 stars, and some old linens.
No one really dines anymore. Breathe
out that rich wood, mahogany reds,
first born in the rain forests of Belize.

I pull my life toward me like these
small brass handles in my palm. I shine
all eight matching legs it stands on, every
doweled angle, each etched crevice
polished with best intentions. A rag
dipped in almond oil. A walnut cracked
open, rubbed on the sore spots. This
is a good way home.

Words Saved to Use in a Poem
after June Melby

1) *pillowcase*: a large pocket to keep dreams,
often pale blue, pink, or winter white. Space
washed colors of sky. But in modern times,
Ralph Lauren times: salmon, garnet, Pacific
blue, slate.

2) *umbrella*: bumbershoot, a Pluviophile's discard,
a nose blown, full of black soot, city of coal. Fires
lit to pardon heady flooding on Saint Anne's Row.
1969.

3) *mulligan*: a do-over, a do unto others better next
time. Even as formal rules deny it, you are given
another chance.

4) *rascality*: fragility, trickishness and guile, a rhapsody
of prosody, a seedling of time, deviltry and memory,
and unmanned booths. Filling up with snow cones and
sun-spun sugar of pink and blue.

5) *aubergine*: o nightshade, flower of the darker side,
color of his shirt. Compline come full circle in silence.
Please don't let another aubade be written from these words.

Reminder Notes to Self on Writing
with words from notes on writing with Maria Irene Fornes, Carmen Fornes, Julie Herbert and John O'Keefe.

Be a renegade!
Sing *Sausalito, Sausalito, Sausalito…*
while walking the wharf.
Sew till your fingers are numb.

Kill the critic in your head.
Avoid making sense at all cost.
Wait…get very quiet.

Listen to your own words.
Taste your syllables.
Allow yourself bias, for God's sake,
just jump off the cutting edge of anywhere
at all. Scare the shit out of yourself.

So, think of someone you want to sleep with
more than you believe it yourself and
look longingly at your words as if they
were that lover on warm moist sheets.

Admit your weakness. Do it for your poetry.
Do it for your life. And then do it again
to see if you can start over once more
and still hold on to your innocence.
Do it again and again. Just to admit

your weakness. Go ahead and write
from this confusion. Find a body
for confusion. Find confusion
in your body. Write the questions.
Let them pay your ransom.

Astronomical Units of Flight

Certain light travels like sunset breakers,
like tide pools painted with a wink
that borrows its crimson hue
from the blood of a running wolf,
its emerald tint from chromium's hot glare.

It knows itself, knotted and tied,
a string
of golden moments
made from briny-spiced diamonds, hanging
around the violet neck of the Milky Way.
This light comes on tiptoe

through glistening rungs in space. It clings
to a feather of truth that tickles its thoughts
from the closet of longing. Dark places
that cover a lover's face, but do not obscure
the sky, or the sentient trail
of an iron salt
across the stain of the moon.

Glorious Tango
after Yannis Ritsos

Please come, my slow dress in a chair.
A place to sit without a chill,
spring has come in the by and by.

Glorious tango of taking off winter coats
and hats, spectacles, elbow-length gloves.
The grace of darkness buried in skin. Later,

the upstairs windows come ajar, bones fly, star
of the sun. Listen to my thoughts at high speed.
Danger is lurking. The one who always asks first

stands in line thumbing yellowed photos.
Stories, conjecture—who we are. Down
in the basement, belly of the house, we know

we must stay, that we always will and were meant to.
Look. This final room: wooden bureau, mirror,
chair; my dress on the floor.

The Dazzling
after Die Erblindende by Ranier Maria Rilke

Is it the way we are changed
whenever sipping tea? Who will be

served first diving into an unknown
cup?   There is so little warning

when change catches hold. Laughter
comes—sometimes not. Is it a crime

the way we smile or raise ourselves
to speak? How can we walk toward

birth without terror? We can imagine
it so. We want to slide into dawn.

But we walk so far behind the others,
eyes lit up like the surface of a sunlit pond

from which we soon may drink. The shadow
turns long, cannot survive just one full

night. And yet with a single gesture,
we see...

Peggy Dobreer is the 2017 winner of the Downey Symphony Orchestra Poetry Matters Prize. Her poems have appeared in numerous journals and anthologies and she is author of *In the Lake of Your Bones* (Moon Tide Press, 2012). A former dancer and movement artist, Peggy teaches E=Mc2Bodied Poetry Workshops in a variety of retreat and literary settings. She was a program director at AROHO2015 A Room of Her Own Foundation, and continues to curate poetry arts events throughout Los Angeles. Find her at www.peggydobreer.com

Acknowledgements

I want to thank the following editors who have included my work in their journals. I have been buoyed by your acceptances, and for the accompaniment you have given these poems. I cherish each literary family:

"The Dazzling," *Pirene's Fountain, A Journal of Poetry,* Vol. 7, Issue 15, 2014, Glass Lyre Press, LLC

"Serving Fresh Fish," Pushcart Nominee, for *Cadence Collective: Year One Anthology*, edited by Sarah Thursday, Sadie Girl Press, 2014

"Scarlet Billows Start to Fade," Featured Poem for The Juice Bar, edited by Lisa Thayer

"Astronomical Units of Flight," Best Poem in Downey Symphony Orchestra's 2016 Poetry Matters Contest.

"Astronomical Units of Flight," *poetry with a dash of salt & a smattering of other poets* edited by d. marlar, Lady Lazarus Press

"Karma as First Mode of Transportation," Poem of the Week, *Poetry Super Highway*, edited by Rick Lupert.

"Is There A Doctor in the House," Featured in *Cultural Weekly*, March 2018

"Retro Causation," upcoming in *Waves Anthology*, A Room of Her Own Foundation

Notes:

"Scarlet Billows Start to Spread" lyrics and title from "Die Moritat van Mackie Messer", composed by Kurt Weill with lyrics by Bertolt Brecht for "Mack the Knife".

"Her Name Was Tiffany or Else It Was Piper" lyrics and music from Kenny Ortega, composed for "Nuclear Gospel" The Intersection Theatre, San Francisco.

I am increasingly thankful to my editor, Eric Morago, for his faith and guidance in urging this manuscript into a book; to Michael Miller, Moon Tide's founder, for publishing my first collection, *In The Lake of Your Bones;* to my teacher and beloved accomplice, Brendan Constantine, for inspiration, belief in my work, cover art and words; to Nicelle Davis for the Poetry Circus, sisterhood and her haunting foreword to this book; to Mandy Kahn and Ricki Mandeville, for their humbling and generous remarks on the cover; to Alexis Rhone Fancher, for seeing me in ways I never would; to my favorite lovebirds, Janet Fitch and Andrew John Nichols, for insightful inspiration, dance retreats and whimsy; to Elena Secota, for always pointing to the moon and the stars; and to my remarkable family, for their (above and beyond) sanctuary and support; to you, dear reader; and to my astonishing daughter, Lena, who keeps it real, all real, all the time.

Patrons

Moon Tide Press would like to thank the following people for their support in helping publish the finest poetry from the Southern California region. To sign up as a patron, visit www.moontidepress.com or send an email to publisher@moontidepress.com.

Anonymous
Robin Axworthy
Conner Brenner
Bill Cushing
Susan Davis
Peggy Dobreer
Dennis Gowans
Half Off Books
Jim & Vicky Hoggatt
Ron Koertge & Bianca Richards
Ray & Christi Lacoste
Zachary & Tammy Locklin
Lincoln McElwee
David McIntire
José Enrique Medina
Michael Miller & Rachanee Srisavasdi
Terri Niccum
Ronny & Richard Morago
Jennifer Smith
Nathan Smith
Andrew Turner
Mariano Zaro

Also available from Moon Tide Press

Junkie Wife, Alexis Rhone Fancher (2018)
The Moon, My Lover, My Mother, & the Dog, Daniel McGinn (2018)
Lullaby of Teeth: An Anthology of Southern California Poetry (2017)
Angels in Seven, Michael Miller (2016)
A Likely Story, Robbi Nester (2014)
Embers on the Stairs, Ruth Bavetta (2014)
The Green of Sunset, John Brantingham (2013)
The Savagery of Bone, Timothy Matthew Perez (2013)
The Silence of Doorways, Sharon Venezio (2013)
Cosmos: An Anthology of Southern California Poetry (2012)
Straws and Shadows, Irena Praitis (2012)
In the Lake of Your Bones, Peggy Dobreer (2012)
I Was Building Up to Something, Susan Davis (2011)
Hopeless Cases, Michael Kramer (2011)
One World, Gail Newman (2011)
What We Ache For, Eric Morago (2010)
Now and Then, Lee Mallory (2009)
Pop Art: An Anthology of Southern California Poetry (2010)
In the Heaven of Never Before, Carine Topal (2008)
A Wild Region, Kate Buckley (2008)
Carving in Bone: An Anthology of Orange County Poetry (2007)
Kindness from a Dark God, Ben Trigg (2007)
A Thin Strands of Lights, Ricki Mandeville (2006)
Sleepyhead Assassins, Mindy Nettifee (2006)
Tide Pools: An Anthology of Orange County Poetry (2006)
Lost American Nights: Lyrics & Poems, Michael Ubaldini (2006)

www.ingramcontent.com/pod-product-compliance
Lightning Source LLC
Chambersburg PA
CBHW031212090426
42736CB00009B/885